THE
SWASTIKA
POEMS

THE
SWASTIKA
POEMS

William Heyen

The Vanguard Press, Inc. / New York

Copyright © 1977 by William Heyen.
Published simultaneously in Canada by Gage Publishing Co.,
Agincourt, Ontario.
All rights reserved.

Library of Congress Catalogue Card Number: 76-39729
ISBN: 0-8149-0780-6

Designer: Elizabeth Woll
Manufactured in the United States of America.

1   2   3   4   5   6   7   8   9   0

The author wishes to thank the editors of the following periodicals, in which certain of these pieces first appeared: *The Carleton Miscellany* ("A Snapshot of My Father, 1928"); *Quarterly Review of Literature* ("For Wilhelm Heyen"); *Modern Poetry Studies* ("For Hermann Heyen"); *The Ontario Review* ("Two Relations," "Lament," "Men in History," "The Liberation Films," "Darkness," and "The Uncertainty Principle"); *John Berryman Studies* ("Riddle"); *The Ohio Review* ("Passover: The Injections" and "The Swastika Poems"); *Rapport* ("I Dream of Justice"); *The Iowa Review* ("A Visit to Belzec"); *Pembroke Magazine* ("On an Archaic Torso of Apollo"); *The Southern Review* ("The Numinous"); *The Humanist* ("Simple Truths"); "For Wilhelm Heyen" and "For Hermann Heyen" also appeared, in different versions, in *Depth of Field* (1970). A shorter version of "Erika" appeared in *Strivers' Row*. "The Trench" was originally published as a broadside by Rook Press.

Contents

The supreme tragic event of modern times is the murder of the six million European Jews. In a time which has not lacked in tragedies, this event most merits that unenviable honor—by reason of its magnitude, unity of theme, historical meaningfulness, and sheer opaqueness. . . . Ultimately, the only response is to continue to hold the event in mind, to remember it. This capacity to assume the burden of memory is not always practical. Sometimes remembering alleviates grief or guilt; sometimes it makes it worse. Often, it may not do any good to remember. But we may feel that it is right, or fitting, or proper. This moral function of remembering is something that cuts across the different worlds of knowledge, action and art.

—Susan Sontag

1/MEN IN HISTORY

A Snapshot of My Father, 1928

His hick tie
flares out into the granular wind,
his thick kraut hair sprouts from under a cap you
wouldn't be caught dead in.

But he's smiling, he's
holding hard to the ship's rail,
and he won't let go because he's on his way now,
he's on his way to America,

a country he smelled
when the North Sea warmed to summer,
a country he saw when the story in a reader said
rivers, trees, land, money.

So he's eighteen, and somehow
he's on his way now. The Atlantic wind
blows his baggy trousers way out in front of him,
and he looks like famine,

this hayseed
with bad teeth, this carpenter

sporting a jacket patched at an elbow, this Dutchman
wearing a new life in his eyes.

But he doesn't know
what he looks like, or doesn't care,
but just cares to hold tight to the rail because
everything is all right,

he's on his way now,
my father, for richer or poorer,
smiling for fifty years now because he's going to make it
to America.

For Wilhelm Heyen

(d. 1940, buried in Holland)

I

The shaft of the film curls with smoke.
Within the camera's depth of field:

battalions of bone-white crosses
(the lines of a chaplain's gestures

in a pre-battle benediction)
and a still-living soldier

fronting them, and staring
into my eyes, into the dark. He waves.

The soldier moves his right arm.
This is, and was, certain in time.

II

The film shakes, and holds.
He chars at the edges, burns,

5

but the film moves. Holland
snows. White-tarpaulined trucks

lumber like polar bears.
Soldiers dig trenches,

stack shells, string
barbed wire with cans, plant

mines. Night falls. The wire
rattles. The mines flower.

III

Because these causes are never just,
rest, my twenty-year-old uncle, rest.

I'll say you walked with soldiers,
killed, were killed. The Dutch

cut the medals from your chest.
That book of love poems

my father said you pressed
out of your heart is also dust.

IV

Wilhelm, your face, a shadow
under your helmet,

6

fades from the gray air
of newsreels. You cannot hear

your nephew try to understand your name.
I've seen you move your arm,

a scythe, a pendulum,
seen your hands cupped full with blood.

These are all your wars.
Asia trembles. You are never dead.

Letter to Hansjörg Greiner

(d. Oct. 20, 1944 at War Camp Arsk, the Urals)

I

Your wife once said
you marched to war
like a boy to school.

There is no rule.
She said no more.
She went to bed.

The American soldier she married,
half to get her children here,
half because he loved her,
still mutters and regrets
your years together.

Listen to a few more
footnotes to the war.
But what would you want to hear?

That your wife, martyred and noble,
welcomes your comrades to your German home?
Your family fled Berlin
down a corridor of flame.

That justice was done?
When the gas dropped in,
scapegoat Jews scratched their appeals
by bloody fingernails
on their shower stalls.

That your Fuehrer is alive and well
and still stands on balconies
waving to crowds?
He died by his own hand,
lives only for those whose histories
keep floating toward them like a cloud
risen from the Nazi furnace.

II

Has no one written you? Then I. You're
another one I don't know how
to talk to, but have to.

Stalingrader, it's now another spring
since the Russian winter
of your capture

and your death soon after.
Nine years ago
I married your daughter. I know
she still sends her love:

Lieutenant, outside our shining windows
the year has turned again.
Hannelore, whom you left
just old enough to know, and who,
now and again during our long winters
fingers the gold locket and bracelet
you gave her, now plants
a bed of flowers,
marigolds and zinnias that will soon

bloom in our yard.
But you will still be dead.

III

Born in America of German immigrants—
a mother who dismisses guilt,
a father whose two brothers
died on your side,
whose graves he has never seen,
whose loss has wrenched him from sleep
all these years to hover speechless
over the beds of his four sons to try
to make them over to Wilhelm and Hermann
in the gracious dark—
I have a stake in this,
so tell me, Lieutenant,

if we could sit and talk,
if we could reach past
your decades of silence,

10

if we could walk the woods today
where maple and ash unfurl
like no flag,
whether, as your last night
fell toward you over the white hills,
you still dreamed of rank, medals,
a hero's return,
or longed for death and the deep snow.

IV

No. You probably wouldn't know.
I suppose you'd stammer and shrug,
recall, if anything, the duel
that slashed your left cheek to the bone,

your marriage, and how it was
you met her, and how it was
to kiss her for the first time,
and how it was to walk the street,
a Wehrmacht officer with three children
whose hair the German sunlight
caressed like a hand.

V

Herr Greiner, this final matter of your sons:
sometimes while walking,
or reading the papers, or driving
in traffic to work, we say your name

to ourselves in the slow syllables of prayer,
construct your face and posture from photographs
or the few moments we remember,
and from thin air.

For a few seconds, we close our eyes.
This is where you live,
in flashes of darkness
under our eyelids.

(1971)

For Hermann Heyen

(d. 1941 over Russia)

Hermann, the Channel was blue-green
when you banked your plane and headed
back. But the Stuka's wing,
down which you sighted the countries you hated,
shone brilliant as medals,
didn't it? Your plane seemed
almost to be on fire, didn't it?

My Nazi uncle, you received the letters
my father still talks and wonders about—
the ones in which he told you to bail out
over England and plead insanity.
You got the letters, didn't you?
But you kept saying you'd land in London
with the rest of your squadron,

in a few months, when the war was over,
of course. Of course. But they needed you
in Russia, didn't they? And the few
who bailed out there were met by peasants
with pitchforks and scythes, weren't they?

Anyway, your plane blew up, for a moment,
like a sun; your dust bailed out all over.

Hermann, I don't mean to make fun.
But this is only a wargame I'm playing,
anyway, isn't it?—pretending you can listen,
or that you matter any more?
Later, past the days your ashes
sifted down through the gray Asian air,
the Allies leveled even Berlin, where,

under his alabaster ruins
your warlord's charred bones
sang hosannas in their sleep.

Hermann, what would you say now
if you could talk? How would you deny
my father's letters? I keep
questioning him. He says: *Ich habe ihm oft
geschrieben, aber.* . . . He is almost sixty
now, and longs for you, and longs
for Wilhelm—buried in Holland, by the way—

more than ever. Your living brother's heart,
so to speak, has empty corridors.
He sleeps back to the day young Wilhelm fell,
and the day you burned,
for a moment, like a sun. He stares
for hours at photographs
of the two of you in uniform.

14

Hermann, my three brothers and I
are the most dispassionate of all Heyens ever.
Though named for Wilhelm, your poet-brother,
I often curse the two of you and spend my hours
writing verses that wonder how your fiery,
German romanticism started,
and where, at last, if it did, it died.

A History of Germany
under National Socialism

Even Carin Goering's ideal
Aryan skull in the rubble.

Men in History

I

Keitel *still* expected the secret weaponry
of deliverance, and maniacal Goering
even *now* angled for power.
Eva Braun, shadowy queen
of this black bower, resigned herself
to long hours of waiting
for cyanide, or one more night's love
no war would rob her of,

but over the Fuehrer's last days,
as Berlin crumbled above him
and a fine dust seemed
to cloud his bunkers, he moved
divisions of ghosts across his maps,
and the others around him
kept asking themselves
whether this was all a dream.

Shriveled, insubstantial, unreal
even to himself, he walked

with an old peasant's stoop
in a uniform stained by food
dropped by his shaking hands.
Above him, his Reich's burnished eagle
lay in rubble, flew downward into flame.

II

But now it was mid-April,
his birthday, his fifty-sixth
year to heaven,
and since it was his last, and since
he knew, he left for the last time
his shelter and eventual tomb—
sixteen feet of concrete and six of earth—
for the Chancellery's upper rooms,

where walls peeled, drapes were down,
and the paintings he'd insisted on
were long since packed away.
A hat lay in an easy chair,
and old newspapers haunted the corridors.
This man shook hands, blustered,
and passed out signed photographs of himself
framed in silver. Often nostalgia

floated him back twenty years until
his eyes brimmed with tears quickly
wiped away with the back of his hand.

18

III

Then it was over.
He took his leave, wound
back down to his bunkers
to finish the war,
to wait for God to open
the iron gate of the sun
for one more soldier soon
to die. This architect, this

messiah, this man in history
would die just once,
would flame just once into a darkness
far past our spit and curses.
As he said to Albert Speer:
"Believe me, it is easy for me
to end my life. A brief moment
and I'm freed of everything."

IV

Born in Brooklyn of German parents, I
have lived with him for thirty years.
I remember lines scratched on our doors,
the crooked swastikas my father cursed
and painted over. And I remember
the *Volksfest* at Franklin Square
on Long Island every summer—
the stands of smoked eel, the loaves

of dark bread, the raffles, the shooting galleries,
the beer halls, the bowling alleys,
the boys in *lederhosen*
flooded by an ocean of guttural German
they never learned, or learned to disavow.
I remember the hourly parades
under the lindens, the elders'
white beards, the sad depths of their eyes.

I remember their talk of the North Sea,
the Rhine of Lorelei, Cologne's
twin towers, the Black Forest,
the mountains, the Hamelin piper
who led everyone's children to nowhere.
But I, too, was a child: all those years
there was one word I never heard,
one name never mentioned.

Two Relations

I

He came to our city,
and the people were shouting and crying.
They hailed the Fuehrer
as the deliverer.
I was in the crowd, caught
in delirium, a moving box,
pushed forward.
Closer and closer he came
in the glistening black car
through a sea of heads.
The people almost touched him,
but I could not lift my arm.
And now he was opposite me,
and he gave me a look.
It was a look of death,
there was the chill of death in his white face.
I knew it, then:
he was the incarnation of death.
I felt it in my marrow.
All those who cried after him as their redeemer,

cried for death.
His look froze my heart,
and I raised my arm,
and I cried *heil*.

II

The small stone house stands by itself,
thirty meters long, thirty meters wide,
five meters high. Two small windows
with heavy bars. A lawn in front,
and a wooden shack, where people undress,
to shower, they think.
They walk into the stone house.

Concrete floor and no furniture.
Maybe two hundred nozzles stick out.
The two windows and door lined with rubber.
It's a shower, all right, but gas comes out,
and twists their bodies into awful shapes.
Gas does not put them quietly to sleep.
Their flesh is torn with their own or others' teeth.

Their bodies were bluish red.
We dragged them out of the gas house
by hair and ears and feet
and threw them on a flat wagon.
Each wagon had room for seventy bodies.

22

We drove the load to the crematorium.
We stacked them at the entrance.

Flesh does not burn like wood—
it takes a long time to burn humans.
Burning seventy or eighty corpses every day—
it's slow going.
There is always a fire in the ovens.
Day and night
a whitish smoke blows out of the chimney.

Riddle

From Belsen a crate of gold teeth,
from Dachau a mountain of shoes,
from Auschwitz a skin lampshade.
Who killed the Jews?

Not I, cries the typist,
not I, cries the engineer,
not I, cries Adolf Eichmann,
not I, cries Albert Speer.

My friend Fritz Nova lost his father—
a petty official had to choose.
My friend Lou Abrahms lost his brother.
Who killed the Jews?

David Nova swallowed gas,
Hyman Abrahms was beaten and starved.
Some men signed their papers,
and some stood guard,

and some herded them in,
and some dropped the pellets,

and some spread the ashes,
and some hosed the walls,

and some planted the wheat,
and some poured the steel,
and some cleared the rails,
and some raised the cattle.

Some smelled the smoke,
some just heard the news.
Were they Germans? Were they Nazis?
Were they human? Who killed the Jews?

The stars will remember the gold,
the sun will remember the shoes,
the moon will remember the skin.
But who killed the Jews?

Passover:
The Injections

Clouds pass over, endless,
black fruit dripping
sap from the branches
of lightning.

We lie down in the field,
thousands of us,
never mind the rain.

Soldiers come toward us,
groups of three or four.
The wind opens their long coats.
Underneath, their uniforms are black.

They bend over to the babies.
The babies cry,
for a little while.

"We are living in Biblical times,"
a woman says.

I Dream of Justice

*In old Prussian law, three categories of thieves are specified: of gold,
of horses, and of bees. . . . It may have been this clarification of
natural law which stirred the mind of the nomad, rousing in him an
inchoate perception of order and continuity.*

—Kay Boyle

I

You who are poor, take back your coins.
You who are Jews, take back your teeth.
You who are shorn, take back your hair.
You who were brave, you who collapsed in terror,
you who are dead, take back all the lost days of sunlight,
for I have hanged the thief of gold.

II

Farmers, back to your herds,
for the steel tanks they sired are lost,
and the sharks that glide under the waters:
cavalry vanished into the red wind,
the tanks flamed back to black ore,
the submarines burst like lungs.
Take back your herds,
for I have hanged the thief of horses.

III

The thief of bees thought,
when your bees swarmed,
they had gathered for battle.
Take back your hives,
which bore him such bitter honey,
for I have hanged the thief of bees.

IV

I have awakened.
What is it I have come to?
Far outside this morning's window
horses graze their meadow,
and the bright air around the trees is strung
with golden necklaces of bees.

The Trench

This is Verdun,
horizon of barbed wires
lit with flares.
Shudder of mortar on both flanks, and now
down the dreamed line the repeated scream:
gas. My thick fingers,
my mask unstraps slowly and heavily from my pack,
a fumble of straps,
buckles, tubes.
I try to hold my breath,
and now the mask is on,
smells of leather and honeysuckle vomit.
The poison smoke
drifts into the trench,
settles. My neck
strains to hold up the mask.
I will.
Behind this pane of isinglass
I am ready,
my bayonet fixed for the first black shape
to fill trenchlight above me and fall.
I know that all my life one

German soldier has plunged toward me
over the bodies of the lost.
I am ready for him.
We are both wearing masks,
and only one of us will live.

Three Fragments
from Dreams

I

It was my own face shining
from the wet orange gables
of medieval Goslar.

II

In Hannover where he lay,
I visited the grave of Leibnitz.
From high above, his face
darkened in the grass
as the square clouds passed.

III

Again I walked that Freiburg corner
under the frieze
where a unicorn has stabbed the air
since Luther. The years

have worn its stone horn
down, down.
Imagine the rains.
Imagine the wars.
How many women?
It's almost impossible to remember.
Imagine the flowers in their hair.

Darkness

Thirty, fifty, eighty years later,
it's getting darker.
The books read, the testimonies all taken,
the films seen through the eye's black lens,
darker. The words
remember: Treblinka green,
Nordhausen red,
Auschwitz blue, Mauthausen
orange, Belsen white—
colors considered
before those places named themselves. Thirty,
fifty, eighty years later. Now
the camps—I lose them—
where are they? Darker.
If it is true
that I've always loved him,
darker. If it is true
that I would kill again,
darker. If it is true
that nothing matters,
darker. If it is true
that I am jealous of them,

the Nazis' hooked crosses, the Jews' stripes,
darker. He
speaks inside me. Darker.
I lie on a table
in the Fuehrer's bunker,
outside his chamber,
in the hall. I am waiting.
They do not see me,
dogs nor people. This
dream begins again, the film
circles and burns. Eighty, fifty,
thirty years. Darker. He
touched my forehead. Darker. He
speaks now, says, somehow,
lower, tells me to speak to the lower power,
for once, to say,
come back, enter, I was once alive.
Darker. The air
swims with words, hair
twines the words, numbers
along a wrist, along
a red brick shower. Darker.
To forgive them,
killer and victim: darker.
Doctor, help me kill
the Goebbels children. Darker.
Across the street, now,
a cattlecar, stalled.
The skin lampshades darken under varnish.
Fragments. Can I call
him back? Darker. Millions still
call him back in deepest prayer,

but the light diffused
as spray, past
Andromeda, in spiral
shadows. Darker, always
darker. *SS*, death's head,
oval hollow deadface hole for boot—
fragments. Darker, the heroes
all dead in the first five minutes.
Darker. To enter
this darkness, to dig
this chancellery garden to my own
remains, to watch
as the black face and scrotum
lacking one egg stare up
at the sun, to speak
with that charred jaw,
carrying this with me. Darker.
Underneath the answer, under
the darkness, this love I have,
this lust to press
these words. Darker. He
tells me *lower*,
and the black breastbone aches with it,
the last black liquid
cupped in the eyesockets smells of it,
odor of cyanide's bitter almond,
the viscera smeared to the backbone
shines with it, for me
to say it all, my
hands around his neck,
mouth to mouth, my lips
to kiss his eyes to sleep. We

will taste this history together,
my reader: take a deep breath.
Take it. Smell
almond in the air.
The leader lives.

2/ERIKA

Erika

*They were points of transit, they offered impressions whose essence
could not be held steady, was always vanishing, and when I inquire
what there is about them that cannot be stressed and found valuable,
to give a firm position in the topography of my life, I keep on coming
up against what keeps retreating from me, all those cities become
blurs, and only one place, where I spent only one day, remains constant.*

—Peter Weiss

Buchenwald: a beech wood, a soft word shining with sunlight falling through yellow leaves. A name, a place of terror.
Ravensbrück: bridge of the ravens, a word out of the medieval
gloom. *Dachau, Auschwitz:* words with no, so far as I know,
particular root meanings, but words that leave us confounded
and inconsolable. And *Bergen-Belsen.* The name whines like a
missile or jet engine. It is a name from which there is no
escape. And it is impossible to imagine what happened at
Belsen.

It happens that my earliest memories are of 1945. I was
five. We lived in Woodhaven, on Long Island. My father
worked in the shipyards, building against the Axis. I remember the green gate in front of our house and what the houses
on our street looked like and how close together they were.
I remember a trellis that leaned against one side of our garage.
I remember, though I did not know what it was at that time,
the persecution we suffered because we were Germans, the
swastikas my father scraped from our windows or painted
over when they appeared suddenly in the mornings on our
steps or doors. 1945. At Belsen, as the trees began to leaf that
spring, Jews and other dissidents were being murdered by
the thousands. I remember the day in 1945 that Franklin

Roosevelt died. I remember that day because my brother and I were getting ready to go to the movies when my mother came outside and said we couldn't go because the President had died and the movies were closed. I remember that day because I was bitterly disappointed. And that day, because Roosevelt had died, down in his Berlin bunker Hitler was pounding his fist on a table and assuring himself that God had sent him a sign, that Roosevelt's death meant the Third Reich would now rise from the rubble. And that same day, children no older than I were being put to death at Belsen.

Belsen is forty miles north of Hannover, out of the way, and was meant to be. You are not likely to visit the place, but if you do, if you find the signs to *Gedenkstatte Bergen-Belsen* and find the place and park in the lot outside the grounds, you will walk under pines past a caretaker's apartment to which the central building, a square and simple affair of glass and stone, is attached. From the outside it looks like a small art gallery, perhaps, or a gymnasium. You will pause outside its glass doors to read a sign whose legend outlines the camp's history.

In 1940 Belsen, an already existing barracks, became a prisoner-of-war camp, Stalag 311. Russian captives were quartered there when a massive epidemic of spotted fever swept the camp. April of 1943 saw the establishment of the so-called Detention Camp Bergen-Belsen; Jews began to be collected there. In March of 1944 people who were no longer able to work were transferred to Belsen from other camps. In October and November of 1944 eight thousand women arrived from Auschwitz-Birkenau. A month later, the latter camp's *SS* Commandant, Joseph Kramer, took charge at Belsen. The camp grew rapidly, apace with his ambition. Within a year after Kramer's arrival the camp grew from fifteen thousand to sixty thousand prisoners, many of whom came from camps too near the front.

Belsen's last year was absolute hell. Nine thousand were executed there during the first two weeks of April, 1945. In the middle of that April the British arrived to liberate the camp, but despite their best efforts conditions were such that an additional nine thousand died during the next two weeks. Eighteen thousand died during that terrible April. While I was playing in the Woodhaven streets, six hundred people a day died at Belsen. The sign outside the memorial building concludes with the estimate that at least fifty thousand had been murdered at the camp. Anne Frank, who wrote that she needed only sunlight to hope, was one of them.

You are not likely to visit the place, but if you do, and if you are there in December, as I was, you will walk inside into a single big room. The room will be dark and cold. You will find no bones, hair, teeth, lampshades made of tattooed skin there, and for this you will be thankful. But you will see a map that locates what were German concentration camps and their surrounding cells and satellites. The map is a spiderweb of camps, stations, deployment centers. Then you will see the photographs that cover the stone walls, images you've seen so often before: the mummified bodies, the Lugers held against the temples of old men, the huge eyes, the common graves from which arms and legs sprout like mushrooms. But this time these photographs are of the very place where you are standing; this is a dimension you have not entered before.

In one photograph smoke rises from the center of the camp above barbed wire and shacks and pines. In another, you will see only the backs of seven women who stand above their graves for a last few seconds of life as the photographer trips his shutter. These are young women who must not have been

41

at the camp for long: their hair seems luxurious, and they are not thin. Their dresses seem to billow slightly behind them, their hair seems slightly blown back from a wind blowing toward the camera. Now, as the seven women stand there above that ditch, their hands bound behind their backs, they can see dozens of bodies below them, perhaps the bodies of their husbands and children. For a few seconds, as the photographer arranged his equipment or simply brought his camera into focus, the women may have glanced up at the sky. They may have spoken to one another. They must have prayed. A few seconds after they stood up in the light and air and wind for a last time, they fell forward into the darkness. They are still falling.

On another wall in this room you will see blow-ups of newspaper descriptions of the conditions the British troops found here in the spring of 1945. They had to burn the place to the ground as quickly as possible because they feared an epidemic. Corpses were hanging out of windows. The dead had to be buried in a hurry. There was no time for more than cursory identification procedures. The machine of the camp had run down as the British had advanced. Records were no doubt being destroyed, no doubt the German officers and guards were making their own plans, no doubt the murder of the last nine thousand they had time to murder those first two weeks in April was an inconvenience. This was Nazi *Kultur*.

You will walk outside past the mass graves. Each grave has a concrete marker: *Hier Ruhen 800 Tote April 1945; Hier Ruhen 1,000 Tote April 1945; Hier Ruhen 2,000 Tote April 1945*. The graves are banked at their bases by a band of about two feet of stone, and then the earth curves and slopes upward, rising as high as your head. The mounds are shaped something like loaves of bread, but squarer, flatter.

You might say to yourself: *They are really here. I am at Belsen, and these are the graves of people who were murdered here. This is the camp at Belsen.*

You will see that the graves are covered, as is the whole area, with Erika. Erika, bell-heather, *heide,* a heath plant, wild and strong. Wild and strong, and beautiful. When not in bloom Erika is green, a deep green. There is a poem by the German poet Hermann Löns, who died at Verdun, that begins: "Grün ist die Heide, / Die Heide ist grün." In December, Belsen is green, a dark green. But in early fall, I am told, Erika blooms a reddish blue or bluish red, and then Belsen must be very beautiful, the sun perhaps occasionally breaking through the cloud cover, a warmer wind perhaps rustling the stiff blooming Erika over the graves, the *heide's* billions of flowerlets veiling the open spaces in shifting mauves and orchids and blue-purple shadows. It must be very beautiful and very terrible at Belsen when each fall the Erika blossoms. I do not think I will ever live a fall day when I do not think of Belsen. I will be driving to work, or opening a window, or playing cards with friends, or reading, and I will think of Erika blowing green or blooming violet-red over the dead at Belsen. And whenever I see a starling, or crow, I will remember the crows that stroke their black wings against the wind at Belsen.

Bergen-Belsen is not a big place, and it isn't old: what happened there happened only about thirty years ago. And it isn't a complicated place. It is very simple. At the edge of the camp there is a shaft of white marble. The words incised on it are simple and direct, and eloquent. Its fifth and sixth words are painted blood-red: Israel and the World *Shall Remember* Thirty Thousand Jews Exterminated in the Concentration Camp of Bergen-Belsen by the Hands of the Murderous Nazis." And further down on the stone: "Earth Conceal Not the Blood Shed on Thee!" Bergen-Belsen is a simple place, but it is more eloquent than the cathedral at Köln. It is a simple place, and it is easy to remember: there may be just a few days a year when the Erika is covered with snow, but in the early fall it blooms in the shades of lilac, the blossom of memory.

And I will always remember speaking to the caretaker at Belsen. He said that he still finds things there. When spring breaks he tills the soil or replaces a brick along a walk or transplants a tree or rakes through the Erika and finds a rusty spoon, or a tin cup, or a fragment of bone, or a strand of barbed wire, or a piece of rotten board, or the casing of a bullet, or the heel of a shoe, or a coin, or a button, or a bit of leather that crumbles to the touch, or a pin, or the twisted frames of someone's eyeglasses, or a key, or a wedding band.

3/THE NUMINOUS

The Tree

Not everyone can see the tree, its summer cloud of green leaves or its bare radiance under winter sunlight. Not everyone can see the tree, but it is still there, standing just outside the area that was once a name and a village: Lidice. Not everyone can see the tree, but most people, all those who can follow the forked stick, the divining rod of their heart to the tree's place, can hear it. The tree needs no wind to sound as though wind blows through its leaves. The listener hears voices of children, and of their mothers and fathers. There are moments of great joy, music, dancing, but all the sounds of the life of Lidice: drunks raving their systems, a woman moaning the old song of the toothache, strain of harness on plowhorse, whistle of flail in the golden fields. But under all these sounds is the hum of lamentation, the voices' future.

The tree is still there, but when its body fell, it was cut up and dragged away for the shredder. The tree's limbs and trunk were pulped at the papermill. And now there is a book made of this paper. When you find the book, when you turn its leaves, you will hear the villagers' voices. When you hold the leaves of this book to light, you will see the watermarks of their faces.

The Baron's Tour

Gaze down at the Rhine.
I remember it red
with Roman blood.
We have always lived in this castle.

This is the room of trophies:
deer, griffin, boar, bear,
the long hair
and leathery scalp of a chinawoman.
Dragon, wolf, lampshade of jewskin.
We have always lived in this castle.

At the base of this stair, a door
opens to the Fuehrer's chamber.
In its center stand
candelabras of eternal flames.

We have thought to leave here,
but the labyrinthine passages,
the sheer plunge to the river,
the stones that have come to caress us . . .

48

This is the hall once lined
by hearts impaled on pikes.
These are the stair rails
of russian bone.
This is the turret
where the books are burned.

Come, see where kings entered
the grained wood of the oak bed
where you will sleep tonight.
One said he'd dreamed

of his whole courtyard filled with heads
whose eyes mirrored
fields inside of fields inside
of fields forever.
We have always
lived in this castle.

Two Walks

I

(Through the Night with My Father, 1945)

One of them is yours, my father said.
I looked, but into too much heaven
for me to find which part was mine.
It's exactly overhead,

and always will be. See it, there,
the one that seems to see you?
He was right. I saw it burning near
(planet born when I was born), and blue.

II

(At Bergen-Belsen, 1971)

Morning, while Erika blew green from mound
to mound, the man who works at Belsen
raked a rusted wire from the ground.
Noon, I walk among the thousands dead, hear

crows cry *rawr, rawr* through the dark air.
I watch them drift to nowhere down the wind,
but see we still throw shadows here, my fathers,
my crows, my black immortal stars.

Blue

They were burning something. A lorry drew up at the pit and de-
livered its load—little children. Babies! Yes, I saw it—saw it with my
own eyes . . . those children in the flames. . . . I pinched my face.
Was I still alive? Was I awake? I could not believe it. . . . Never
shall I forget the little faces of the children, whose bodies I saw
turned into wreaths of smoke beneath a silent blue sky.

—Elie Wiesel

    To witness, **to**
  enter this
essence, this
silence, this
  blue, color
  of sky, wreaths
    of smoke, bodies
  of children blue
in their nets
of veins: a lorry
  draws up at the pit
  under the blue sky where
    wreaths rise. These
  are the children's bodies, this
our earth. Blue. A lorry
draws up at the pit
  where children smolder. The sky
  deepens into blue, its
    meditation, a blue
  flame, the children
smolder. Lord of blue,
blue chest and blue brain,

a lorry of murdered children
draws up at the pit. This
happened, this
happens, Your
sign, children
flaming in their rags, children
of bone-smolder, scroll
of wreaths on your blue
bottomless sky, children
rising wreathed
to your blue lips.

The Liberation Films

Seeing the films:
now we begin to know.

A bulldozer working the piles of dead together,
its treads hacking horizontal ladders

into this remorseless German dirt
that translates flesh into Erika and flowers:

now we begin to know.
Now we begin to know.

Seeing the dozer's curved blade curl
the dead like a flesh wave

as high as our heads
toward great necessary pits;

seeing the bodies white
with necessary lime;

seeing the bodies fall
over the graves' edges;

54

seeing the eyes staring at nothing,
the bodies falling in slow motion;

seeing the stick limbs falling in slow motion:
now we begin to know.

Seeing the dead roll and fall
as though flailing their last air,

without words, without sound,
without one syllable of their last prayers:

now we begin to know You, Lord.
now we begin to know.

The Spire

Wherever I am, I am not supposed to be here. I am above the street, above cobblestones shining the black shine of night and rain. It is cold, but in this dream I cannot feel the cold, and wherever I am, I know, I have been here a long time. Great dark shapes hang in the air behind me. Bells. A spire, a fretwork of porous red stone rises above me. Bodiless, I am in the belltower of the cathedral above the square at Freiburg. I have been here for centuries. I am breathing the air that flows around the still clappers of the great bells. The square below is empty. I have lived in this air, I know, since before the spire.

Something is about to happen. A straining of ropes, chains. The bells' clappers begin to slam against cold iron. It is as though the bells are inside of me, as though they are echoing deeply and mournfully the sounds for dead, dead.

It is winter here, a drizzle of sleet sifting through the dark red fretwork of the spire, through the sound of the bells. In the east, toward the forest, the horizon whitens with dawn. Lord, help me, I cry, and awaken.

56

Lines to My Parents

(Hannover, 1971–72)

I

A few days ago,
I saw those Bremerhaven graves.
Unadorned stones
honor our simpler dust.

I almost knelt to save
a leaf of ivy. I even heard
the dead were glad
that I'd returned.

But will you understand?
I was content to watch
the North Sea's wind
wearing away our names.

II

Will you understand?
Canes and armless coats
haunt these German streets
I force myself to walk.

Factories smoke the sky,
and in the absurd cause-
effect of night,
I lie half-asleep

dreaming of thirty years ago.
Below my windows
old soldiers tap the cobblestones,
stop, stare into the mist-

white air; widows
who have worn their weeds
for thirty years, hurry
to nowhere in the steady rain.

III

Last night, at last, I met him,
inside a glade of oaks,
and touched his iron helmet,
and scratched his mossy face.

I stepped inside a clearing,
I walked the hallowed ground.
I found an iron soldier where
a drumbeat seemed to roll.

Nor consecration, nor cathedral,
nor clouds that Jehovah wove,
but rain beat down like shrapnel
through the dead leaves.

Say he drives the wind, father,
say he stares from the sun.
Say he cries like the crows
beating the sky at Belsen.

Say his tears are the rain, mother,
say I have been his brother.
Say his medals are the moon,
say you have been his lover.

IV

My thirty-
first birthday broke with sun
and dried the counter-
clockwise whirl of water

down the drains:
I walked the woods again,
but now alone
in the pine, oak,

and linden autumn.
Once more the leaves
had turned to flame;
gray doves

weighed down the highest limbs;
rabbits burst
across my paths
as they do at home.

V

Say he is molded from nothing, mother,
say he is nowhere.
Say he has not returned,
say he will never.

Say that your brothers died, father,
say that they never lived.
Say you cannot read the writing
below his metal head.

Say he is in the bells, bells,
echoing down the air.
Say he haunts the Erika, father,
forty miles from here.

Say when I hear the bells, mother,
from forty miles away,
they say the Jews have risen
from where the forests burn.

Say that their war is over, mother,
say that his war is over.
Say that your war is over, father,
say that my war is over.

A Visit to Belzec

I

This is Belzec,
in the East of Poland,
in the Lublin region
where the fumes of Sobibor,
Maidenek, and Treblinka still
stain the air:
smell the bodies
in the factories' smoke,
smell the sweet gas
in the clover and grass.
This is Belzec
where the death compound's gate
proclaims in Hebrew,
"Welcome to the Jewish State."
This is Belzec.
This is *SS* humor.
Curse them forever
in their black Valhalla.

II

*"At 7:20 a.m. a train arrived from Lemberg with 45 wagons
holding more than 6,000 people. Of these, 1,450 were already dead on arrival. Behind the small barbed-wire windows,
children, young ones, frightened to death, women and men.
As the train drew in, 200 Ukrainians detailed for the task
tore open the doors and, laying about them with their leather
whips, drove the Jews out of the cars. Instructions boomed
from a loudspeaker, ordering them to remove all clothing,
artificial limbs, and spectacles. . . .*

*"They asked what was going to happen to them. . . . Most
of them knew the truth. The odor told them what their fate
was to be. They walked up a small flight of steps and into the
death chambers, most of them without a word, thrust forward
by those behind them."*

III

Reader, you have walked
into the smoke-streaked mirror
of my dream, but I can't,
or won't remember.
Did my jackboots gleam?
Did I fill out quotas?
Was it before, or after?
Did I close those doors,
or did I die?

I can still feel
iron and cold water on my fingers.
I remember running
along the bank of a river,
under trees with full summer
stars in their branches,
the sky lit up with flares
and the slight murderous arcs of tracers,
the night air wet
with the sugary odors of leaves.
Dogs barked.
Were they mine?
Were they yours?
Was I running from,
or after?

IV

"Inside the chambers SS *men were crushing the people together. 'Fill them up well,'* [Hauptsturmführer *Christian*]
*Wirth had ordered, '700 or 800 of them to every 270 square
feet.' Now the doors were closed. . . .*

*"The bodies were tossed out, blue, wet with sweat and urine,
the legs soiled with feces and menstrual blood. A couple of
dozen workers checked the mouths of the dead, which they tore
open with iron hooks. Other workers inspected anus and
genital organs in search of money, diamonds, gold, dentists
moved around hammering out gold teeth, bridges and
crowns. . . ."*

V

Reader, all words are a dream.
You have wandered into mine.
Now, as workers rummage among the corpses,
we will leave for our affairs.

This happened only once, but happened:
one Belzec morning, a boy in deathline
composed a poem, and spoke it.
The words seemed true, and saved him.
The guard's mouth fell open to wonder.

Reader, we have walked together
into the smoke-streaked
terror of Belzec,

and have walked away.
                    Now wind,
and the dawn sun,
                    lift our meeting
to where they lift the human haze
                    above that region's pines.

On an Archaic Torso of Apollo

(after Rilke)

We cannot experience that storied head
in which Apollo's eyeballs ripened like apples. Yet
his torso glows, candelabra by
whose beams his gaze, though screwed back low,

still persists, still shines. Or else his breast's
curve would never blind you, nor his loins'
slight arcs smile toward center-god, where
sperm seems candled from under.

Or else this stone would squat short, mute, dis-
figured under the shoulders' translucent fall,
nor flimmer the black light of a beast's pelt, nor

break free of its own ideas
like a star. For here there is nothing nowhere
does not see you, charge you: You must change your life.

Other Men in History

Berlin, the *Kaiserhof*, a few years ago:
"If only Paulus had broken out!"
The speaker's brown beer flashed red
as the blood that melted snow at Stalingrad.

"We'd still have had them by their throats!"
Others at his table nodded.
"Now they are all dead, dead,
three hundred thousand of our finest *SS* studs."

The Numinous

Our language has no term that can isolate distinctly and gather into one word the total numinous impression a thing may make on the mind.

—Rudolf Otto

We are walking a sidewalk
in a German city.
We are watching gray smoke
gutter along the roofs
just as it must have
from other terrible chimneys.
We are walking our way
almost into a trance.
We are walking our way
almost into a dream
only those with blue
numbers along their wrists
can truly imagine.

Now, just in front of us, something
bursts into the air.
For a few moments
our bodies echo fear.
Pigeons, we say,
only an explosion
of beautiful blue-gray pigeons.
Only pigeons that gather

over the buildings
and begin to circle.

We are walking again, counting
all the red poinsettias
between the windowpanes
and lace curtains.
It was only
a flock of pigeons:
we can still see them
circling over the block buildings,
a hundred hearts
beating in the air.
Beautiful blue-gray pigeons.
We will always remember.

Lament

(after Rilke)

O how everything deceives,
like my star
of black light, dead
in the heavens
for thousands of years!
I break into tears
at the cold words
from the boat of stars
that passes over, and over.
Where in my body
does the same clock beat?
I would like to walk
away from my heart.
I would like to pray
under the dead sky,
if there were one star
which does not lie,
which endures,
a white city
at the end of its beam,
forever.

The Uncertainty Principle

I

Lord, must this end in prayer, or
does the Lord enter secular words?
What is in the wind? Does the wind's
red trail ever end? What is certain?
By the time Jacob Bronowski walked
into the pond—is it Your pond?
is it our pond?—what had he learned?

II

Through a whole hour of film
I'd watched Bronowski's eyes:
his glasses flashed
as though his brain were bare to sunlight.

The camera swung past tables of skulls
gathered in Göttingen by Blumenbach
over a hundred years ago:
from these bowls of old bone rose

a column of Nazi
science, calipers, iron
maggots, monographs
building ovens
to precise human
specifications.

I'd listened to Bronowski's voice
following what Rilke, speaking
of Apollo's torso called
"allen seinen Randern,"
all of its contours that broke open the atom
only to wonder, a tolerance, a
smiled estimate of error, a
limit to light to render, a
melting, a wavery withholding, what
Heisenberg won to, something like
Quine's "radical translation," language or
particle physics flying from
earth to the stars we will
worry forever.
               Still,
Erwin Schrödinger spat on his black-
shirt assistant's boots.

III

We pass beneath the connected iron arch
that still insists *Arbeit Macht Frei*
to the sky at Auschwitz,
pass to where Bronowski stands

dressed in a suit of his ideas, wearing
a black tie, stands at the edge of the pond
here in Auschwitz into which, as he says,
the ashes of millions "had been flushed,"

pass to where he stands almost
in a dream of his ideas here at the edge
of this pond in Poland, stands as though
at the ditch of his own death, says
"It was arrogance, dogma, ignorance that did this,"
and walks into the pond. The sun

candles his face, birdsong
trills from somewhere behind him.
Bronowski walks toward us, toward
the camera into the pond, bends over,
kneels, cups water in his right hand,
cups in his hand the mud, the residue of ashes,
bows here in the pond at Auschwitz.

IV

of this pond Lord
of this pond of all ponds
of silence these
words from water this
mist's gray
radiance these
first rays of the solar ovens'
undigested yellow gristle these
corridors catching the sunlight these

weeds' twist these daily
shifts these clouds this
smoke drifting waters' surfaces these
sounds escape these
voices escape I can
almost hear I
can almost hear I
cannot hear these
columns of shadows this
evening this

night now again wind
moaning past its pads'
curled edges past
its lilies' red-black
blooms its
only tongues

V

Maybe Bronowski knew that he would do this,
would walk toward the camera into the pond,
but we could not know that he would do it,
would stand in the shifting mud of the dead,
would help us to touch the watery lives of the dead,
would break the iron beat of our minds to a flutter,
a chance, would say, once and for all this
only truth that will not murder, as human
smoke rises into the blue air of Auschwitz,
would say that the atoms escape, the pond lives,
the mind's only border is this blur of tears.

73

Simple Truths

When a man has grown a body,
a body to carry with him
through nature for as long as he can,
when this body is taken from him
by other men and women who happen to be,
this time, in uniform,
then it is clear he has experienced
an act of barbarism,

and when a man has a wife,
a wife to love for as long as he lives,
when this wife is marked with a yellow star
and driven into a chamber she will never leave alive,
then this is murder,
so much is clear,

and when a woman has hair,
when her hair is shorn and her scalp bleeds,
when a woman has children,
children to love for as long as she lives,
when the children are taken from her,
when a man and his wife and their children

74

are put to death in a chamber of gas,
or with pistols at close range, or are starved,
or beaten, or injected by the thousands,
or ripped apart, by the thousands, by the millions,

it is clear that where we are
is Europe, in our century, during the years
from nineteen-hundred and thirty-five
to nineteen-hundred and forty-five
after the death of Jesus, who spoke of a different order,
but whose father, who is our father,
if he is our father,
if we must speak of him as father,
watched, and witnessed, and knew,

and when we remember,
when we touch the skin of our own bodies,
when we open our eyes into dream
or within the morning shine of sunlight
and remember what was taken
from these men, from these women,
from these children gassed and starved
and beaten and thrown against walls
and made to walk the valley
of knives and icepicks and otherwise
exterminated in ways appearing to us almost
beyond even the maniacal human imagination,
then it is clear that this is the German Reich,
during approximately ten years of our lord's time,

and when we read a book of these things,
when we hear the names of the camps,

when we see the films of the bulldozed dead
or the film of one boy struck on the head
with a club in the hands
of a German doctor who will wait
some days for the boy's skull to knit, and will enter
the time in his ledger, and then
take up the club to strike the boy again,
and wait some weeks for the boy's skull to knit,
and enter the time in his ledger again,
and strike the boy again,
and so on, until the boy, who,
at the end of the film of his life
can hardly stagger forward toward the doctor,
does die, and the doctor
enters exactly the time of the boy's death in his ledger,

when we read these things or see them,
then it is clear to us that this
happened, and within the lord's allowance, this
work of his minions, his poor
vicious dumb German victims twisted
into the swastika shapes of trees struck by lightning,
on this his earth, if he is our father,
if we must speak of him in this way,
this presence above us, within us, this
mover, this first cause, this spirit, this
curse, this bloodstream and brain-current, this
unfathomable oceanic ignorance of ourselves, this
automatic electric Aryan swerve, this

fortune that you and I were not the victims, this
luck that you and I were not the murderers, this

76

sense that you and I are clean and understand, this
stupidity that gives him breath, gives him life
as we kill them all, as we killed them all.

Ewigen Melodien

Something: dead friends' welcoming whispers? but
     something: wooden windbells, chimes? but
something: my skin soft now Lord we are all dead but

something: music lower than birdsong but
     something: our throats that screamed are soft now and
something: thrum of dew drying from grassblades? but

something: our fingers that clawed are soft now and
     something: rustle-of-grain sound somehow yellow? but
something: our lungs that burst with blood are soft now and

something: trees filling with windsong? but
     something: deep cello timbre, low resinous hum? but
something: jaw muscles soft now, neck muscles, tongues but

something: brain hymn, bodiless heartbeat? but
     something: we should have known this
something: . . . the melodies begin . . .

The Swastika Poems

They appeared, overnight,
on our steps, like frost stars
on our windows, their strict
crooked arms pointing

this way and that, scare-
crows, skeletons, limbs
akimbo. My father
cursed in his other tongue

and scraped them off,
or painted them over.
My mother bit her lips.
This was all a wonder,

and is: how that sign
came to be a star flashing
above our house when I dreamed,
how the star's bone-white light

first ordered me to follow,
how the light began

like the oak's leaves in autumn
to yellow, how the star now

sometimes softens the whole sky
with its twelve sides,
how the pen moves with it,

how the heart beats with it,
how the eyes remember.

NOTES

The quotation from Susan Sontag is from her discussion of Rolfe Hochhuth's play *The Deputy* in *Against Interpretation* (New York, 1966). . . .

"Dutchman" ("A Snapshot of My Father, 1928") was a term used by Americans to label all those immigrants, including Germans, who sounded as though they spoke Dutch. The word often carried more than a little of "The Fool" with it. . . .

"Stalingrader" ("Letter to Hansjörg Greiner") was the general term used for anyone who took part in that battle. Greiner, before volunteering for or being ordered to the Russian front, worked at the Propaganda Ministry in Berlin. After finishing this poem, I found him listed as one of about fifty participants at Goebbels' almost daily conferences from 1939–1941 (*The Secret Conferences of Dr. Goebbels*, ed. Willi A. Boelcke, New York, 1970). . . .

The rubble in "A History of Germany under National Socialism" is the rubble of Goering's Prussian estate. *The Reich Marshall*, by Leonard Mosley (Garden City, 1974), though too sympathetic to Goering, captures the cloying Aryan melodrama of the Carin-Hermann relationship, from their first meeting in a Swedish castle until her skull is kicked up in the ruins of the mausoleum he had built for her. . . .

Much of "Men in History" is based on Albert Speer's memoir *Inside the Third Reich* (New York, 1970). . . .

"Two Relations": Saul K. Padover was an American intelligence officer in psychological warfare who moved into Germany immediately behind our armies. These two stories, the first by a German woman who had once seen Hitler at Aachen, and the second by a Frenchman who was forced to work at Sachsenhausen in 1944, are adapted from Padover's *Experiment in Germany* (New York, 1946). . . .

I wrote "Passover: The Injections" after reading Susan Fromberg Schaeffer's powerful and moving novel *Anya* (New York, 1974). . . .

"Darkness": Lev Bezymenski's *The Death of Adolf Hitler* (London, 1968) describes the autopsies performed on charred bodies dug up by the Russians from the Chancellery garden. In *Adolf Hitler* (New York, 1973), Colin Cross argues that the Russian findings, particularly in regard to the body supposed to be Hitler's, are disputable. . . .

The epigraph from Peter Weiss for "Erika" is from "My Place," an essay about a day he spent at Auschwitz (*German Writing Today*, ed. Christopher Middleton [Baltimore, 1967]). . . .

"The Tree": Lidice was a Czechoslovakian village entirely destroyed by the Nazis in 1942 in reprisal for the assassination of the area's Gestapo "Protector" Reinhardt Heydrich by Czech patriots. All males of fifteen or older were shot; women were sent to concentration camps; physically acceptable children were Germanized while the others were also sent to camps. The village, in effect, disappeared. . . .

Sections II and IV of "A Visit to Belzec" are taken from Richard Grunberger's *Hitler's SS* (New York, 1972). . . .

"The Uncertainty Principle": Willard Van Orman Quine is the author of *Word and Object* (Cambridge, Mass., 1960), a study of the possibilities of precise communications through language. The quoted phrase suggests to me that our individual meanings for words are various and even eccentric enough to require constant and strenuous translation as we try to reach one another. . . .